MINDFULNESS

A Guide to Reducing Anxiety and Stress

Diane Gimpel

San Diego, CA

Printed in the United States

For more information, contact:
ReferencePoint Press, Inc.
PO Box 27779
San Diego, CA 92198
www.ReferencePointPress.com

LIBRARY OF CONGRESS CATALOGING-IN-PUBLICATION DATA

Author: Diane Gimpel
Title: Mindfulness: A Guide to Reducing Anxiety and Stress
Description: San Diego, CA : ReferencePoint Press, 2026.
Includes bibliographical references and index
Identifiers: LCCN 2025014583 (print) | ISBN 9781678210922 library binding | ISBN 9781678210939 ebook

For compete cataloging-in-publication data please go to www.loc.gov.

CONTENTS

Living in the Moment

Sean Grabowski was a guy who experienced anxiety—thoughts of fear and worry that got in the way of his life—but he relied on his passion—snowboarding—to help relieve it. That worked until he was twenty-five, when a snowboarding accident left him with torn ligaments in his knee and the inability to clear his head by playing sports. As depression set in, Grabowski looked for help. He found it in a book titled *The Power of Now* that urged readers to live in and focus on the present instead of the future. Grabowski's journey toward mindfulness began there. "Mindfulness has helped me to be more productive, and it has helped me to update my self-image and belief system software to be a better version of myself," Grabowski wrote on his website, the Mindful Steward. "I still experience challenges, and stressors, just like everyone else, but with my new skillset, I combat them differently than before. It has helped me broaden my horizons, and it has improved my physical and mental health."[1]

"Mindfulness has helped me to be more productive, and it has helped me to update my self-image and belief system software to be a better version of myself."[1]

—Sean Grabowski, anxiety sufferer

The Definition of Mindfulness

Mindfulness occurs when people are able to experience their feelings, sensations, and the environment in the present without judging those things as right or wrong. At the same time, those who are being mindful steer their thinking away from thoughts about the past or future. By doing that, people free themselves from thinking negative things over and over. Sometimes people go to therapists to get guidance on how to be mindful, and sometimes people learn to do it on their own, perhaps by reading about it, as Grabowski did.

Mindfulness can be experienced through everyday living. In other words, people do not have to stop what they are doing to be mindful. They can experience mindfulness while driving or working or cleaning or eating. However, sometimes people *do* stop what they are doing to become mindful. One way is through a specific kind of meditating. That practice is called mindfulness meditation. That is often what comes to mind when people think of mindfulness.

Mindfulness as a specifically named practice has been around since the 1990s but has become better known in recent years. One sign of this is the increase in the number of times people have searched for the term on the internet. Searches for the term

People do not have to stop what they are doing to be mindful. They can experience mindfulness while driving, working, cleaning, or eating.

mindfulness steadily increased from 2004 and peaked in April 2020, which was when the COVID-19 pandemic hit. People had high anxiety about the new disease and about reactions to it, like schools and businesses shutting down. Another gauge of interest in mindfulness is the fact that millions of people buy mindfulness apps. Young adults especially like those apps, according to a 2023 study published in the journal *JMIR Mental Health*. The data-gathering site Statista notes that the greatest percentage of users of such apps (21 percent) are ages eighteen to twenty-four. However, because many studies and statistics do not differentiate between meditation and mindfulness, it is difficult to say precisely how many people practice mindfulness specifically.

Criticism of Mindfulness

Although mindfulness is helpful for many people, the practice has been the subject of some criticism. Mindfulness is a nonreligious practice. However, some argue that it cannot be separated from its origins in Buddhism, which is one of the world's major religions. Other critics cite studies that suggest that mindfulness has had negative effects on the mental health of children who practiced it. Still others warn that practicing mindfulness is not a substitute for therapy, even though some people use it that way. Finally, some critics say mindfulness leads to a kind of selfishness.

That is what David Atashroo, a medical doctor, talked about in a LinkedIn post. During a summer day in Las Vegas, Nevada, Atashroo was on an airplane that became very hot inside because takeoff was delayed. Atashroo became physically uncomfortable. To cope, he turned to his mindfulness training and focused without emotion on work he was doing rather than on his negative emotions about the heat. That worked for him, but then someone in the airplane had a seizure. After helping the person, Atashroo criticized himself because he had not acted sooner. He noted, for instance, that he could have asked flight attendants to hand out water to help other passengers cope with the heat. He wondered whether such action would have prevented his fellow passenger from becoming ill. “I learned that my tranquil inner-peace offered no comfort to anyone but me,”[2] Atashroo says.

Positive Outweighs Negative

Although some have criticized the practice, the National Institutes of Health highlights the positive effects of mindfulness. It contends that mindfulness can help people make healthier choices, reduce anxiety and depression, lower blood pressure, improve sleep, and increase pain tolerance. “Studies suggest that focusing on the present can have a positive impact on health and well-being,” the institutes said in a June 2021 article. “Mindfulness-based treatments have been shown to reduce anxiety and depression. There’s also evidence that mindfulness can lower blood pressure and improve sleep. It may even help people cope with pain.”[3]

The positive effects of mindfulness, therefore, lead many to embrace it. Although mindfulness has been the subject of criticism, scientists and practitioners continue to advocate it as a tool people can use to help alleviate stress and anxiety when done properly.

Experiencing and Coping with Stress and Anxiety

Ellis Edmunds is a psychologist who helps people battling unrelenting anxiety, something he knows about from personal experience. He struggled with anxiety as a teen. "Meeting new people, pursuing a romantic interest, or just giving a presentation for a class was a big struggle," Edmunds wrote on his website. "I would jitter, sweat, and just be awkwardly nervous in any sort of social or performance situation. Anxious thoughts would keep me up at night and I was very hard on myself."[4] Edmunds uses mindfulness meditation to reduce his anxiety, and he teaches mindfulness techniques to the clients of his psychology practice who are seeking similar relief.

"Meeting new people, pursuing a romantic interest, or just giving a presentation for a class was a big struggle. I would jitter, sweat, and just be awkwardly nervous in any sort of social or performance situation. Anxious thoughts would keep me up at night and I was very hard on myself."[4]

—Ellis Edmunds, psychologist

Prevalence of Stress and Anxiety

Anxiety is the sense of dread or worry a person feels when experiencing stress, so the two go hand in hand. Stress, at its most basic, is a response to pressure, whether that is physical pressure on the body or emotional pressure in the brain. People often think of stress as something experienced emotionally. A first date, a school project, a big test, and trouble at home are examples of events that often lead to emotional stress. That type of stress usually goes away when the event that caused it ends.

Stress is common. Forty-nine percent of Americans feel stressed on a regular basis, according to Gallup, a company that conducts polls. Chronic stress happens when a stressor lasts a long time—like a bad relationship or a bad job. If the stressor ends but the anxious feelings will not go away and become excessive, the person experiencing those feelings may have developed an anxiety disorder.

The most common mental disorder in the world is anxiety disorder. More than 300 million people worldwide—nearly equal to the population of the United States—have an anxiety disorder, according to the World Health Organization. People with these disorders experience intense and excessive fear and worry. In the United

Stress is common. Many adults experience stress on a regular basis. If someone is under stress for a long period of time, it can lead to an anxiety disorder.

States alone, about 40 million people age eighteen or older—for perspective, that is more than the number of people who live in California—have an anxiety disorder.

The Brain's Experience of Stress and Anxiety

Among those with an anxiety disorder is Becki, who was diagnosed when she was eighteen. "I used to get stressed very easily at school and would feel physically sick on exam days," she says. "I am also sensitive to loud noises and struggle to be in crowded spaces for long periods of time."[5] As time went on, Becki experienced panic attacks, which are episodes of physical symptoms like sweating, chest pains, and a racing heartbeat accompanied by intense fear. She also had bouts of insomnia—the inability to fall asleep or stay asleep. Becki's symptoms were a sign that her body's response to stress was not working properly.

Medication for Anxiety

People who have anxiety have a number of things they can try for relief. Mindfulness is one of them. Others include physical activity, socializing, deep breathing, and psychotherapy. Sometimes, however, those efforts do not trigger the desired results. In such cases those with anxiety may go to a doctor to get a prescription for medication.

Many medications exist for anxiety. They trigger the brain to release various chemicals—neurotransmitters known as dopamine and serotonin—that are responsible for feelings of happiness. However, as is the case with most medications, antidepressant and antianxiety drugs can come with side effects. Furthermore, as with any prescription, sometimes people have to try several different medications before they find the one that works best.

Additionally, a study published in 2023 by *JAMA Psychiatry* showed that mindfulness is just as effective at treating anxiety as a certain common anxiety drug. Mindfulness-based stress reduction "was shown to be a well-tolerated treatment option with comparable effectiveness to a first-line medication for patients with anxiety disorders," the study reports.

Elizabeth A. Hoge et al., "Mindfulness-Based Stress Reduction vs Escitalopram for the Treatment of Adults with Anxiety Disorders," *JAMA Psychiatry*, 2023. https://jamanetwork.com.

When a person feels stress, the body reacts with what is commonly known as the fight-or-flight response. The fight-or-flight response is a survival mechanism that helps people react quickly to something that threatens their safety. Here's how the fight-or-flight response works: The brain responds to stress by signaling the release of a hormone called epinephrine (also known as adrenaline), which increases the heartbeat and breathing. Epinephrine also causes senses to become sharper and the brain to become more alert. In addition, the brain signals the release of glucose—sugar—and fats into the bloodstream so the body has fuel for its fight against the threat or its retreat from it. If the brain thinks the threat is continuing, another hormone—cortisol—is released in the body to make sure the body remains alert. The system goes into overdrive when the body reacts to actions that appear to be life threatening.

The fight-or-flight response to stress is, in itself, not a bad thing. Under dangerous circumstances, the body's response can help ensure survival. However, if the threat continues—for example, if someone lives in a violent neighborhood or in a house with abusive people—the stress and the response to it can last a long time. This can be damaging to the body.

Some people experience this bodily reaction even when they do not face life-threatening events. When this occurs, the person might feel a generalized sense of anxiety that is not rooted in any specific peril. In such cases, the survival mechanism has gone awry and, as it does for those who constantly face threats of physical or emotional violence, the stress response becomes damaging.

Stress and Anxiety Symptoms

Stress and anxiety have similar symptoms. They include feeling overwhelmed, being unable to fall asleep or stay asleep, restlessness, impaired concentration, muscle tension, irritability, anger, nausea, diarrhea, headaches, sweating, changes in appetite, and increased heart rate. In Sophia's case, anxiety led to insomnia.

Stress and anxiety have similar symptoms. They can include feeling overwhelmed, which can lead to being unable to fall asleep or stay asleep.

The problem began for Sophia during the summer when she was about twelve. She was able to sleep only two or three hours each night. "I always thought it might have had to do with some of my first early experiences with anxiety,"[6] Sophia says. Her anxiety spiked during the summer, so that was when she struggled with sleeping. During the school year she was less anxious and could sleep better.

Eventually, however, insomnia plagued Sophia during the school year, as it did Haley Tiffany, who also suffered with many of the other symptoms associated with anxiety, including nausea, panic attacks, and lack of concentration: "In class I change my position many times in my desk," Tiffany says, describing what it is like wanting to be able to pay attention in one of her high school classes but not being able to do it. She continues:

> I cannot sit still. My mind wanders off into so many places. *Wait? Did she just call my name?* I fiddle with my pencil, carving my name into it with my finger nails. Oh no . . . pencil broke. I can't get up to use the pencil sharpener. *What if it*

doesn't work? What if everyone looks at me? "Does anyone have a pen?" We start taking notes. I'm copying anything she writes on the board, but around my notebook page I sketch flowers with vines along the margin. I shouldn't be doodling in class at my age, but I can't help it.[7]

Physical Effects of Stress and Anxiety

As Sophia and Haley Tiffany experienced, stress and anxiety can take a toll on health. The physical responses mounted by the body to protect itself from harm are not supposed to be maintained by the brain indefinitely. Experiencing the fight-or-flight response persistently, which keeps adrenaline moving through the bloodstream, can damage blood vessels and arteries, raise blood pressure, and cause heart attacks and strokes. In fact, some experts say stress is as much of a risk factor for heart disease as smoking, lack of physical exercise, excessive drinking, and obesity are.

Speaking of obesity, which can lead to heart disease, the cortisol released during the fight-or-flight response increases appetite. An increased appetite can make people eat more. Cortisol also leads the body to store more unused nutrients as fat. In other words, while one of the body's responses to stress and anxiety can be a loss of appetite, the body also can respond with increased appetite and weight gain. Both can hurt health.

In some cases, even short-term stress can cause significant health problems. One such problem is called takotsubo cardiomyopathy. The condition involves the weakening of the main pumping chamber of the heart. When this occurs, it can cause a person to experience chest pain so strong that it feels like a heart attack. The person also can experience shortness of breath, dizziness, and lightheadedness. The condition is the result of a severe emotional or physical stressor, like the loss of a loved one. That is how the condition gets its nickname: broken-heart syndrome.

Consequences of Unhealthy Stress Management

Sometimes the ways people deal with stress and anxiety can lead indirectly to long-term health problems. That happens when people use drugs or alcohol or other unhealthy means to manage their emotions. "When people feel they cannot escape the circumstances of their chronic stress, they may cope by turning to unhealthy behaviors," says Allison Gaffey, a Yale Medicine psychologist who specializes in cardiology—the medical specialty that focuses on the heart. "We know that stress is associated with behaviors such as unhealthy diet, smoking, and increased use of alcohol."[8] Those behaviors can lead to high blood pressure, obesity, and other conditions that are bad for heart health—as well as addiction.

Martin turned to alcohol when he was fourteen to cope with anxiety and became addicted. "It took me a long time to realize that drinking too much was the way I dealt with my crippling anxiety and depression," he wrote on a blog. "When I drank, everything felt easier. I felt happier and like I was better at socializing."[9] After Martin recovered from a serious illness when he was fifteen and his anxiety spiked, so did his drinking. By the time he went to college, he was drinking vodka alone in his room. His parents sent him to rehab. It took a second rehab stint when he was twenty-one before his recovery took hold.

Managing Stress and Anxiety in Healthy Ways

Because of the short- and long-term damage stress and anxiety can cause the body, it is important to learn how to manage them in a healthy way. A person can combat the physical symptoms of stress or anxiety by triggering the body's relaxation response—the opposite of the fight-or-flight response. There are many ways to do that, many of which people can do on their own at no cost.

One such way to trigger the relaxation response is through deep breathing. To do this, a person breathes in very slowly through the nose until the lungs cannot hold anymore and then

Stress-Related Diseases

Chronic stress, meaning stress that is continuous and long lasting, can lead to an anxiety disorder. It also can lead to conditions including high blood pressure, diabetes, and arthritis.

The brain chemicals released during stress cause the heart to beat faster, which causes the blood to push with greater pressure against the arteries that carry blood throughout the body. This is usually a temporary condition. But when a person experiences chronic stress, the brain responds by continually releasing those same chemicals. This strains the blood vessels, which can cause them to narrow. The result is that vital organs will not get the nutrients they need and can be damaged. This type of damage can cause strokes and heart attacks.

The release of stress-related brain chemicals also triggers the body to release blood sugar—glucose—to boost energy levels to cope with a threat. A hormone called insulin works to absorb the extra blood sugar. When stress is long lasting, extra glucose continues to be released, but insulin cannot get rid of it all. That can lead to diabetes, a disease characterized by high blood sugar. Having that much unneeded blood sugar can damage the eyes, heart, brain, and kidneys.

exhales very slowly through the mouth until the lungs are as empty as possible. Why does this work? When the fight-or-flight response is triggered, the body breathes faster and more shallowly so it can take in more oxygen quickly to prepare to act, like run away. By breathing more slowly and deeply, the brain gets the message that there is no threat and no need for a fight-or-flight response.

Another way to combat a fight-or-flight response that has gone haywire is to try visualizing a peaceful scene. The idea is to think about the place as real, three-dimensional, and stimulating to all five senses. In other words, visualization involves exploring not only what the imaginary scene looks like but also how each element smells, feels, tastes, and sounds.

Physical Activity

Scientists say physical activity of any kind is good for reducing stress and anxiety and improving the health of mind and body.

Movement makes the body produce brain chemicals called endorphins that reduce stress and enhance mood. Movement also makes a person focus less on anxious thoughts and helps bodily systems like the digestive system work at their best.

One form of physical activity with benefits for both mind and body is yoga. Like mindfulness, yoga originated in ancient Asian religious practices. Nowadays in the United States, yoga typically is not part of a specific religious practice. Rather, it is used to improve physical strength, balance, and flexibility as well as to calm the mind. Physical postures or poses, deep breathing, and meditation are all elements of yoga.

Many studies have shown the benefits of yoga practice for mental and physical health. According to the National Center for Complementary and Integrative Health, a 2020 review of twelve scientific studies of yoga found that the practice helped people feel less stressed. While that review involved scientific studies of how yoga affected adults, science has shown yoga benefits younger people, too. A 2020 article published in *Frontiers in Pediatrics* found that yoga "generally leads to some reductions in anxiety and depression in youth."[10]

Yoga worked for Jolanthe De Konig, who was so stressed when she was working on her doctor of philosophy degree that she developed chest pains and insomnia. She started practicing yoga at home by using an app and found relief of her symptoms. She says she "was amazed at how focusing on the movements and sensations in my body allowed my mind the breathing room it needed. I realized that I'd been living mostly in my mind and had lost touch with my body."[11]

Like yoga, tai chi originated in Asia and includes breathing, meditation, and movements. Unlike maintaining a yoga position, tai chi focuses more on gentle, flowing movement from one position to another. Because tai chi involves focusing on breathing and movement as they are happening rather than on thoughts, it can help reduce symptoms related to anxiety and depression.

Engaging with People and Enjoyable Activities

Just as the body releases mood-enhancing endorphins after physical activity, it also releases endorphins when people socialize. "In essence, heightened perceived social support corresponds to increased positive affect and diminished anxiety and depression symptoms,"[12] according to a 2024 article written by Evelyn Acoba in *Frontiers in Psychology*. In other words, socializing tends to reduce stress and increase feelings of happiness.

Socializing, physical activity, yoga, tai chi—these are things a person can do to relieve stress and anxiety and also can be counted as hobbies. Other healthy hobbies—like knitting, reading, baking, making art, and listening to music—likewise can help improve a person's emotional and mental health. "Engaging in fun recreational activities helps us avoid boredom and burnout, both of which can lead to depression," says Svetlana Famina, a Kentucky

Hobbies like baking can help improve a person's emotional and mental health by distracting them from negative thoughts.

psychiatrist. "Hobbies distract us from negative thoughts, which may generate negative feelings that lead to mental illness. . . . They help us unwind from the stressful day and calm our minds, therefore decreasing anxiety. They also keep us in a good physical and mental shape, which improves body image and self-esteem."[13]

Giving and Gratitude

While doing things for oneself can relieve stress and anxiety, so can being thankful that good things exist. Feeling gratitude combats the negative thinking that feeds depression and anxiety. Feeling grateful can involve focusing on the present—thinking about something good that happens, even on a bad day, rather than on bad things that happened in the past or worries about bad things that might happen in the future. Also, feeling grateful triggers the brain to release dopamine and serotonin—the chemicals associated with feelings of happiness—and keeps in check the release of cortisol—the chemical associated with the fight-or-flight response.

> **"Engaging in fun recreational activities helps us avoid boredom and burnout, both of which can lead to depression."[13]**
>
> —Svetlana Famina, psychiatrist

Giving does the same thing, triggering the brain to release dopamine and serotonin, as well as oxytocin, a chemical that makes people feel connected to other people. "When we do things for other people, it makes us feel much more engaged and joyful," says Susan Albers, a psychologist. "That's good for our health and our happiness."[14]

Getting Professional Help

Although giving, feeling gratitude, socializing, physical activity, and hobbies can relieve feelings of stress and anxiety, sometimes people cannot get enough relief with those measures alone. Sometimes they need the help of mental health professionals like social workers, counselors, psychologists, and psychiatrists. Professionals can train patients to relax, often coaching them on various strategies like deep breathing and visualization. Additionally, professionals can use psychotherapy, also called talk therapy and psychoanalysis, to listen to their patients explain their mental health struggles and then train their patients to cope with those challenges by using new ways to think about them. Among the types of therapy are mindfulness-based approaches in which the therapist coaches the patient to focus on the present rather than the past or future, often through the use of mindfulness meditation.

Mindfulness, as it turns out, is the objective of many approaches to managing stress and anxiety. That may be a reason why mindfulness, as a practice, has been the focus of attention in recent years.

The Basics of Mindfulness

Tatiana Posada had a habit of worrying about the past. She was especially anxious about taking tests because, in the past, test taking had been a problem for her. Her worry that she would do as poorly on tests in law school as she had done in her undergraduate studies led Posada to accept her law school's offer of mindfulness training. Her first law school exam became the first test on whether the training had helped her become mindful enough that the stress and anxiety would decrease. She says:

> I remember sitting for my first final, Civil Procedure I. When I opened the exam, I saw that the fact pattern was about seven pages long and involved confusing cases in Florida and Georgia. I could feel my anxiety rise: my heart rate elevate; my breathing intensify; and my body tense. So, I closed my eyes, took several deep breaths, and told myself I was ready: I did everything to prepare. I know the material, and when I open my eyes I am going to read, outline, and write until time is called. And I did just that. And, even better, when I left the testing room, I left the test in there. I didn't ruminate on what I did write, what I didn't write, what I could have written. That was the past and that was where it would stay. This would have been impossible for me to accomplish before mindfulness.[15]

Posada had learned to focus on what was in front of her during the test, rather than worry or think too much (ruminate) about what she might not know or how badly she had performed on tests in the past. She was also able to leave the test without worrying about what mistakes she may have made.

Mindfulness is touted as a way to manage stress and anxiety by training the brain to focus on what senses are perceiving in the moment rather than on intrusive and perhaps negative thoughts about the past and future. For many people, wishing something had happened differently in the past or worrying about something that may or may not happen in the future adds to anxiety. Advocates contend that mindfulness actually changes the brain in a positive way. Aside from reducing stress and anxiety, it can also reduce conflicts with others and result in better focus at work and in school.

Origin of Mindfulness

Mindfulness is not a religious practice, although it arises from the world religion known as Buddhism. Buddhism was founded in Asia in what is now Nepal around 500 BCE. Buddhists believe

Mindfulness trains the brain to focus on what the senses are perceiving in the moment. When taking a test, focus on what is in front of you, rather than worrying about your past performances on tests.

human souls cycle through birth, death, and rebirth over and over unless they become enlightened. On the path to enlightenment is the idea of *sati*, or the "moment to moment awareness of present events,"[16] according to an explanation given on the PsychCentral website. Following the path to enlightenment involves following the example of the Buddha—Siddhartha Gautama, the originator of Buddhism—who achieved enlightenment through meditation.

As Buddhism grew it remained an Asian religion, and today the vast majority of Buddhists live in Asia. Buddhism arrived in America with Asian immigrants who came to build the railroads in the nineteenth century, but its ideas did not spread beyond the Asian communities at that time. During the middle of the twentieth century, when ideas outside of the traditional mainstream caught on with some Americans, Buddhism also caught on with people outside of Asian communities in the United States.

In 1979 a Massachusetts doctor named Jon Kabat-Zinn, who had training in Buddhist meditation, separated the meditation techniques from the religious and cultural aspects of Buddhism. He used meditation to help hospital patients cope with chronic physical pain. He conducted scientific studies to gather evidence to prove his idea worked. He also determined that mindfulness helped not only with physical pain but also with emotional pain. This discovery led Kabat-Zinn to create an eight-week program called Mindfulness-Based Stress Reduction. He is considered by many to be the founder of modern mindfulness because he took Buddhist meditation techniques and combined them with science. Once Kabat-Zinn created his nonreligious mindfulness program, meditation and mindfulness became known as two different things, although the terms often are used interchangeably.

Although Kabat-Zinn's work on mindfulness began in the late 1970s, it was not until the 1990s that mindfulness became more well known. Part of the reason its appeal increased at that time is that it was being researched, so scientific studies were available to show the validity of the practice. It also was becoming the subject of books, news articles, and documentaries.

The Mindful Brain

For those who routinely practice mindfulness, the positive effects come from brain changes. Specifically, experts say, practicing mindfulness regularly changes the distribution of activity among the brain's various networks.

The brain has several networks, each with a specific job. Mindfulness decreases activity in a network that is responsible for ruminating about things that are not happening in the moment. Ruminating thoughts can tend to loop around and around, over and over again. Mindfulness increases activity between a control network that decides which brain network should be working at any given time and the rumination network. Scientists say that means the control network becomes better able to control the rumination network while it makes attention networks—the networks whose job it is to make the brain pay attention to the senses in the moment—get busy. As a result, the brain spends less time thinking about things in the past or the future and more time focused on the present. "Mindfulness training can help change

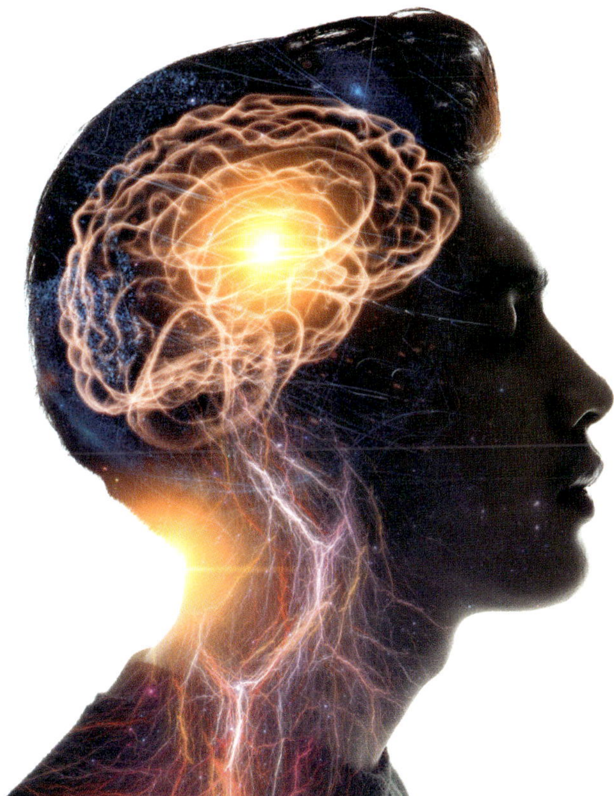

The brain has several networks, each with a specific job. Mindfulness decreases activity in the network responsible for ruminating about things that are not happening in the moment.

patterns of brain activity because the synapses within these attentional networks can strengthen or weaken with use,"[17] says McLean Bolton, a researcher at Max Planck Florida Institute for Neuroscience. In other words, a person who feels less stressed and anxious with mindfulness would continue to practice it, which would lead to brain changes.

How Mindfulness Helps

The changes in brain activity happen as a result of people becoming aware of their thoughts and then choosing which thoughts to focus on. When people choose to focus on what they are experiencing in the moment without judging it, then the brain cannot bombard them with repeating thoughts about bad things from the past or worries about the future.

Mindfulness and Chronic Pain

More than 50 million Americans report having to cope with chronic pain. Pain is considered chronic when it lasts for more than three months. People typically take medicine to cope with pain. Scientific studies show mindfulness can help, too.

In a study published in 2023 in the journal *PAIN*, scientists found that mindfulness meditation changed people's response to pain. They determined that people who engaged in mindfulness meditation were able to break a link between a part of the brain that registers pain from the part of the brain that reflects on things. This decoupling allowed people to experience physical pain without an emotional response to it. As a result, study participants who practiced mindfulness meditation experienced a 33 percent decrease in pain. "Mindfulness meditation is one way to change the way stimuli are perceived and can provide improvements in stress, anxiety, sleep, and pain," says Robert W. Gereau, a professor of anesthesiology at Washington University School of Medicine.

Nonetheless, mindfulness does not solve chronic pain. "There is no cure for chronic pain nor is there one silver bullet therapy," says Fadel Zeidan, who was one of the researchers for the 2023 study. Zeidan says mindfulness should be used in conjunction with other methods of pain management.

Quoted in Clarissa Brincat, "Mindfulness Meditation Changes How the Brain Processes and Perceives Pain," Medical News Today, July 15, 2022. www.medicalnewstoday.com.

Additionally, because people take time to process their thoughts while practicing mindfulness, they stop reacting immediately and impulsively to those thoughts. When people are "in the moment," they tend to watch their thoughts, not react to them. Not reacting to thoughts can keep people from doing something they might regret. Impulsive actions that end badly can cause stress because they can hurt relationships. They also can cause stress because they add more to the loop of negative thoughts. Dan Harris, a former ABC News anchorman who left the news business to do a mindfulness podcast and work on a mindfulness app, says:

"You can kind of understand mindfulness as a quality of self-awareness that allows you to see how chaotic your mind is without getting carried away by it."[18]

—Dan Harris, mindfulness app creator

> You can kind of understand mindfulness as a quality of self-awareness that allows you to see how chaotic your mind is without getting carried away by it. We have this rushing river of thoughts and urges and emotions, but we don't have any visibility into this nonstop cacophony in our minds, and because we don't see it clearly it just owns us most of the time. And mindfulness is a way to kind of step out of the Matrix and to see how wild the mind is—to see the contents of your consciousness so that you don't get carried away by it.[18]

Choosing what thoughts to focus on also helps reduce the activation of the fight-or-flight stress response. That response happens automatically when the brain senses a threat—even when that threat is a bad experience from the past or worry about the potential for something bad to happen in the future. If a person stops focusing on those thoughts, the stress response is not triggered.

Mindfulness can help people treat themselves better and reduce negative self-talk. Jasmine Abriel used to tell herself every day that she was not a good enough person after she scrolled through social media and saw lots of people who seemed like they knew what they wanted and were comfortable with who they were. "I hated how I looked, felt, and lived," she says. "I hated how no matter how hard I tried, I couldn't get to the place where everyone else was."[19] These feelings persisted for years, until she decided to change her negative mindset by beginning a mindful one instead. To make the change, she created worksheets for herself to help her think about, and then redirect, her thinking. The worksheets had daily reminders for her to examine her thoughts and practice mindfulness in some way. For example, the worksheet challenge on Tuesdays was to set aside thirty minutes to practice mindfulness. On Fridays the worksheet told her to ask herself how she could be mindful about loving herself that day.

Mindfulness on the Job

Mindfulness can help people do better at work. That is what happened for Tariq Maonah, an executive at Citibank. For one thing, Maonah said practicing mindfulness helped him make better decisions because his emotions were no longer piloting his choices. Additionally, he said he had more confidence because he was able to bounce back from setbacks more quickly. Similarly, he was better able to cope with change. Finally, he said mindfulness helped him become nicer to the people he worked with and worked for, reducing the opportunities for conflicts with others. "Increasing my self-awareness has helped me to understand my thoughts better," Maonah says. "In doing so, I am able to be more empathetic towards others by displaying appreciation, gratitude and acts of kindness more often."[20] Understanding his own thoughts through mindfulness allowed Maonah to focus less on himself and more on understanding the feelings, thoughts, and experiences of other people.

Another person who found her work life to be better after practicing mindfulness was Jo, a lawyer who suffers from anxiety and depression. Jo found her job to be consuming all of her time—leaving nothing for herself and her family. When she was diagnosed with diabetes, she started working part time. However, she

Mindfulness in Schools

In the wake of burgeoning struggles that students faced from the isolation and anxiety stemming from the COVID-19 pandemic, society has focused a lot of attention on the mental health of youth. To help young people with these challenges, the Centers for Disease Control and Prevention (CDC) recommended in 2023 that schools train their students to use mindfulness. "We know that our teenagers and adolescents are really strained in their mental health," then-CDC director Dr. Mandy Cohen said. "There are real skills that we can give our teens to make sure that they are coping with some big emotions."

The United States does not require school-based mindfulness programs, so no government agency exists to register how many schools are using it. However, various companies that provide such programs have self-reported on their use. One school-based mindfulness program known as Inner Explorer is used in more than one hundred US school systems. Another program, called Mindful Schools, worked with 245 schools during the 2022–2023 school year. Calm Classroom has provided mindfulness training in more than one hundred schools in Chicago and its suburbs. MindUP, a mindfulness program from a foundation created by actress Goldie Hawn, has been used in seventy-three schools worldwide, including schools in New York City.

Quoted in Sharon Johnson, "More US Schools Are Taking Breaks for Meditation. Teachers Say It Helps Students' Mental Health," Associated Press, August 4, 2024. https://apnews.com.

did not know how to manage her thoughts and take care of herself after years of not doing so. She found that mindfulness helped her do that. Jo says:

> For me, it provides small moments which allow me to let go of whatever stress I have been holding onto, because of a complex project, or too much on my plate, a difficult discussion and has helped me be more focused, less reactive and ultimately a better lawyer, as well as a better colleague. I am more in touch with myself and my needs and can recognise when I need to ask for help, as well as manage my mental health conditions more easily. . . . Mindfulness practices help turn down the volume of my internal to do list and find balance in life. . . . It is just carving out a few minutes of my day where I check in with myself and give myself permission to just be.[21]

Science supports the idea that mindfulness can help people in workplace settings. "Mindfulness was associated with lower perceived stress and higher work engagement," states a 2021 study published in *Frontiers in Psychology*. "These findings support mindfulness as a potentially protective and modifiable personal resource."[22]

Mindfulness at School

If the work is schoolwork, mindfulness can help there, too. It can help students reduce stress, anxiety, and the compulsion to revisit the same things over and over in their mind. This frees up brain space for learning. "When kids reduce their symptoms of anxiety through mindfulness, they develop an attitude of curiosity toward their troubles and can think more clearly,"[23] says Nikki Rose, a licensed clinical social worker at the Mayo Clinic Center for Safe and Healthy Children and Adolescents.

An elementary school in Florida gave its students mindfulness training, with apparent success. One student said, "The mornings that I do it is so I can cope and, like, have a good day."[24] Another student talked about how mindfulness can help reduce conflicts between students. "It can help you, like, relieve the stress so you're not angry and you don't take it out on somebody else,"[25] that student said.

"When kids reduce their symptoms of anxiety through mindfulness, they develop an attitude of curiosity toward their troubles and can think more clearly."[23]

—Nikki Rose, licensed clinical social worker

In Nantucket, Massachusetts, second-grade student Sally Laurencelle found that her mindfulness lessons from school could also be useful at home. This came up one night at the dinner table when Sally's older sister, Gabrielle, started screaming and crying following a disagreement with their brother. Sally's father describes his younger daughter's response: "Cool as can be Sally said, 'Gabrielle, you need to take a deep breath and clear your pre-frontal cortex. You'll feel much better.'"[26] The prefrontal cortex is the part of the brain that handles decision-making, emotional regulation, and impulse control. Gabrielle, who had gotten the same lessons in mindfulness at school as her younger sister had, knew what Sally was talking about and what to do.

Mindfulness in Sports

In addition to helping at school and on the job, mindfulness also can help with sports. It can improve athletic performance and lower the risk of developing anxiety, according to a January 2023 study published in the *International Journal of Environmental Research and Public Health*.

Dana Rettke, an Olympic silver medalist who plays professional volleyball in Turkey, benefited from mindfulness training from a

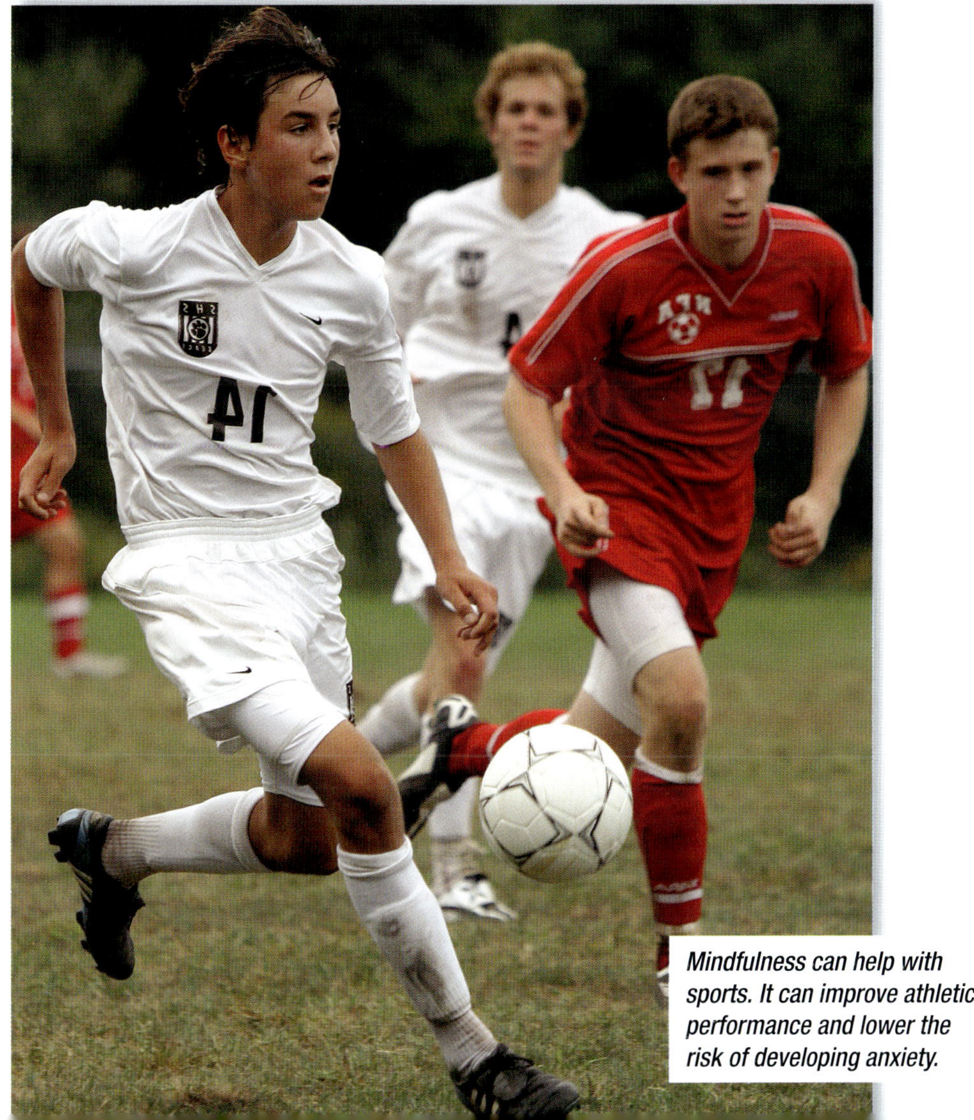

Mindfulness can help with sports. It can improve athletic performance and lower the risk of developing anxiety.

full-time meditation specialist when she was All-American at the University of Wisconsin–Madison. She says she believes more colleges would be likely to provide mindfulness to their student athletes if they knew about its benefits. "This is such an up-and-coming field," she says. "Not a lot of people know about it. Not a lot of people know the benefits of it. Not a lot of people know what it means. If people knew more about it, it would be a huge hit. It's going to spread like wildfire once people really understand the benefits it could have for athletes."[27]

Other Benefits of Mindfulness in Daily Life

People who have coped with anxiety and depression for a long time often work with doctors who prescribe medication to ease their symptoms. Although many people benefit from medication, some worry about the side effects or the prospect of taking these drugs throughout their lives. This was something Shelley La Hay worried about. She decided to look for other ways to manage her anxiety and depression. After attending a neighborhood program on mindfulness, she decided to adopt the practice. "It helped me cope with stressors including people who ask me personal questions about why I'm in a wheelchair," La Hay says. "It taught me how to breathe through anxious moments. It taught me to be kinder to myself."[28]

Adam Kemp, an American who plays professional basketball in Europe, turned to mindfulness to help him cope with Tourette's syndrome. This is a central nervous system disorder that causes involuntary tics like repeatedly making noises or shrugging shoulders. "Practicing mindfulness has not only helped me manage the tics themselves, but it has also helped me with becoming more self-confident with my tics and worrying less about how others view me due to them,"[29] Kemp says.

People of all ages, and in different settings, have used mindfulness strategies to retrain their brains to focus less on the past and the future and more on the present. The effort has helped them manage not only stress and anxiety but also how they view themselves and how they relate to other people.

CHAPTER THREE

Mindfulness Is Not a Cure-All

David Robson turned to mindfulness meditation after coping with anxiety off and on for decades. Sometimes it would work, and the inner voice that got in the way of him thinking clearly and living his life would become quiet. Other times, however, Robson would become more stressed after he tried focusing his mind on the here and now than he was before he began. His heart would beat faster and, rather than negative thoughts from the past being reduced, Robson would be bombarded with those thoughts. "I had assumed I was just uniquely bad at taming my thoughts,"[30] Robson says. He believed this until he came across a study showing it is not uncommon for those who meditate to have some sort of unpleasant experience while they are doing it.

Some of those bad reactions go away quickly the moment a person stops doing the mindful activity that triggered the bad reaction. However, sometimes the bad reaction lingers even after the mindful practice is stopped. Therefore, while mindfulness may help relieve some mental health problems, the practice is not a fix for all of them or for everyone. In fact, it can create problems even though it is a viable tool for managing stress and anxiety.

Mindfulness Can Lead to Unexpected and Unwelcome Effects

Until recently, many scientific studies regarding mindfulness and meditation did not mention or did not include research

Mindfulness may help relieve some mental health problems, but it is not a fix all for everyone. Although it is a viable tool for managing anxiety, it can create problems if not used correctly.

about the negative and adverse effects related to the practice. The study Robson referred to was conducted in 2019 by European and American researchers who surveyed more than twelve hundred experienced meditators online and found that 25.6 percent "reported having had particularly unpleasant meditation-related experiences, which they thought may have been caused by their meditation practice,"[31] according to the researchers.

Another study that investigated how common adverse effects were in mindfulness meditation specifically was published in November 2021. One of the researchers in that study was Willoughby Britton, a neuroscientist who has taught mindfulness and is an instructor in both mindfulness-based stress reduction and mindfulness-based cognitive therapy. Britton also founded a nonprofit organization called Cheetah House that helps people recover from the adverse effects of meditation.

The 2021 study included ninety-six people who had participated in mindfulness meditation programs to cope with depression, anxiety, and stress. More than half—58 percent—reported to the researchers that they had some sort of bad side effect.

Thirty-seven percent experienced a negative effect that disrupted their daily functioning. Six to 14 percent of those in the study had bad effects that lasted longer than a month. Most of the longer-lasting effects had to do with lower energy levels and with dissociation, which is a feeling of being disconnected from oneself, one's emotions, and the environment. Those lasting bad effects tended to happen to people who meditated for more than an hour a day over several days in a row.

A Way to Look at Negative Effects

Although people who practice mindfulness can have bad reactions to it, meditation practice in mindfulness-based programs has negative effects at about the same rate as other psychological treatments, according to Britton. For example, the percentage of people in the study with lasting bad effects from mindfulness meditation is similar to the 5 to 13 percent of those who have undergone psychotherapy and experienced lasting negative effects.

Negative side effects are undesirable, but they happen with a lot of things people do to improve their health. For example, sometimes when people take over-the-counter pain medication like acetaminophen to relieve pain from a headache or reduce a fever, they develop an upset stomach from the medicine. The same thing can happen with measures people take to improve their mental health. The measures may produce an overall positive result but also may have some unwanted side effects. In other words, mindfulness meditation can have some bad effects and still have a good outcome overall. "For people in this study, [mindfulness] had a massively positive effect for depression," Britton says. "You can have positive effects and negative ones at the same time in the same person, and a negative effect can be a positive one at different times."[32] In addition, some unpleasant experiences during mindfulness meditation are normal, like low-level anxiety or fear.

"You can have positive effects and negative ones at the same time in the same person, and a negative effect can be a positive one at different times."[32]

—Willoughby Britton, neuroscientist

Adverse Effects

While some people who are in the midst of a mindful activity can experience a fleeting, unpleasant side effect, some others may experience a negative effect after they have finished a mindful activity. That is called an adverse effect. Adverse effects are results that negatively affect a person's life after the person has ended a mindfulness activity, and those effects last for a while.

Although the adverse effect shows up after the mindfulness activity has ended, the mindfulness activity may or may not have been the cause of the adverse effect. In other words, adverse effects are not the same thing as harm. Harm happens when a treatment *causes* a continuing decline in a person's ability to function or puts the person in a worse condition than he or she was experiencing before treatment began.

Among the adverse effects associated with mindfulness is something called hyperarousal. Hyperarousal is an overstimulation of the brain's response to stress. Hyperarousal is the opposite of what mindfulness is supposed to do. When people expe-

Hyperarousal is the opposite of what mindfulness is supposed to do. When people experience hyperarousal, they become anxious and panicked.

rience hyperarousal, they become anxious and panicked. They may have trouble sleeping. If they have been traumatized in the past, they may feel as if they are experiencing that trauma again, even if the trauma happened a long time ago. That is what happened to Holly Elmore, who says on her blog that she "overdid it with mindfulness and meditation." When she used mindfulness to relax, she panicked. "I'm naturally quite neurotic and highly sensitive to threat, so I suspect that mindfulness training made me perceive lack of awareness as a threat condition,"[33] Elmore says. Neurotic people tend to be anxious—or always on mental alert for something bad to happen—because they think of worst-case scenarios a lot and they doubt themselves. Elmore suggested that when her mindfulness practices turned off her awareness of those worst-case scenarios, her brain registered that as a problem, so her anxiety became worse instead of better.

Hypoarousal

The opposite of what Elmore experienced also can be an adverse effect of mindfulness. It is called hypoarousal. People who experience hypoarousal might not feel their emotions as strongly as they used to. They might even feel like they are not experiencing what is really happening. That is called dissociation. The brain does that sometimes to cope with stress or even boredom. Daydreaming is an example of dissociation, as is highway hypnosis, in which a person drives to a destination but cannot remember getting there. While that may not sound so bad, sometimes it can be. A woman named Louise felt this separation from her body when she was on a meditation retreat. When she got home, she could not get out of bed and her body felt numb. "Her husband took her to the doctor, who referred her to a psychiatrist,"[34] writes Dawn Foster of the *Guardian* newspaper. Louise is not the only person who has felt this way after practicing mindfulness. "We've had an overwhelming number of people contacting the lab and saying, 'I can't feel anything, I don't feel any love for my family. What do I do?'"[35] Britton said in a BBC article.

Some people can experience both hyperarousal—anxiety and panic—and hypoarousal—the numbing of emotions and dissociation—as an adverse effect of mindfulness practices. That is what happened to a woman named Claire, who went on a mindfulness retreat as part of her job. First, she felt pleasantly relaxed, "but then I found I felt completely zoned out while doing it," she says. "Within two or three hours of later sessions, I was starting to really, really panic."[36]

Selfishness

Another adverse effect for some people who practice mindfulness is that it can make them more selfish. If a person is doing something to reduce the focus on emotions and feelings—such as feelings of properly placed guilt—then that might make the person care less about others. "Cultivating mindfulness can distract people from their own transgressions and interpersonal obligations, occasionally relaxing one's moral compass,"[37] says Andrew Hafenbrack, assistant professor of management and organization at the University of Washington. In other words, sometimes negative feelings like guilt and regret are useful in leading people to think about how their actions impact others. People who do not have those feelings might stop caring about whether they hurt others by what they say or do.

Another reported adverse effect of mindfulness is substance abuse. For example, Claire says she became addicted to alcohol when the mindfulness she practiced during her work retreat triggered bad childhood memories. However, mindfulness is far more often seen as a way to reduce substance use disorders rather than as a trigger for them.

Another reported adverse effect is depression. In 2022 British and American researchers studied mindfulness training given to almost eighty-four hundred youths ages eleven to thirteen in a United Kingdom school program. Researchers found that the training led to a very small increase in depression risk for students who had been previously determined to be at risk for men-

How to Avoid Potential Downsides

As mindfulness has been practiced more, scientists have studied negative reactions some people have from doing it. Various ways exist both to cope with negative effects and to avoid them.

For one thing, people should learn about mindfulness before practicing it. Being informed will allow new practitioners to understand negative reactions they might have. They will also have realistic expectations of what mindfulness can accomplish.

Additionally, duration is a risk factor for bad effects. Too much mindfulness can lead to being overwhelmed by things that stimulate the senses or being underwhelmed by emotions. Jon Kabat-Zinn, who developed mindfulness-based stress reduction, recommends forty to forty-five minutes of mindfulness meditation a day.

Some people might find that mindfulness meditation is not the right approach for their emotional wellness. "We should really honor the diversity of contemplative practices that are available, because they all do different things, and people would have a much better chance of matching what they need, if they had a bigger buffet of choices," says neuroscientist Willoughby Britton.

Finally, those who practice mindfulness need to be aware of their moods changing for the worse. In such cases they should ask for help from a mental health practitioner.

Quoted in David Robson, "How Too Much Mindfulness Can Spike Anxiety," BBC, February 4, 2021. www.bbc.com.

tal health problems. The program also resulted in worse social, behavioral, and emotional functioning for some of the students. The researchers concluded the school-based mindfulness training program that was studied should not be offered universally to all adolescents.

Why Are There Adverse Effects to Mindfulness?

Clearly, although mindfulness is helpful for many, it can be unhelpful and perhaps even hurtful to some. One reason for this is that practitioners may be focusing more on awareness than on acceptance. Proper mindfulness requires not only being aware of what the senses are experiencing in the present but also accepting those experiences without judging them as good or bad.

Similarly, when thoughts of the past or future intrude during mindfulness, a person is supposed to acknowledge those thoughts without judging them as good or bad and then return to present awareness. In other words, a person practicing mindfulness is supposed to be a nonjudgmental observer. Those who experience adverse effects from mindfulness tend to have difficulty looking at their thoughts without judgment. "Evidence is accumulating that cultivating the awareness component of mindfulness without the associated acceptance component may lead to unwanted outcomes," says Jamie Gruman, a founding member of the Canadian Positive Psychology Association. "This finding is consistent with other studies showing that the quality of self-focused attention is instrumental in determining whether it leads to well-being or distress."[38]

In addition, mindfulness can be overdone. In other words, too much of a good thing can be bad. People who do a lot of mindfulness meditation tend to be the ones who report long-term adverse effects.

Moderation, therefore, is key. Balance is important, too. The things people do during mindfulness to make their brains behave

When to Go to Therapy

Although mindfulness can help people manage the symptoms of anxiety or depression, it is not a cure for those mental health challenges, nor is it the only or best way to treat them. Sometimes people need treatment from mental health professionals.

People who feel depressed or anxious typically try on their own to relieve their symptoms. Some people try to improve their diet and increase their physical activity. Others talk about their feelings with loved ones. Some people try mindfulness practices. However, those things are not always enough. In fact, a sign that therapy is in order is that a person has tried things to feel better and those things have not brought needed relief.

It is important to seek counseling when symptoms of anxiety and depression grow. Symptoms of anxiety include heart palpitations, stomach problems, irritability, and insomnia. Symptoms of depression include lack of interest in things that used to be interesting, guilt, hopelessness, and tiredness.

differently can lead to unwanted results when one part of the brain or other is cranked up too much. For example, mindfulness aims to activate the part of the brain that will allow people to focus on sensing things without judgment and without emotion. That is good when activating that part of the brain helps a person reduce hair-trigger anger. If that part of the brain is overactivated, however, it can lead people to feel their feelings and emotions less. Similarly, paying attention to the senses through mindfulness can be good when it gets people to stop focusing on bad things that happened in the past or worrying about what bad things might happen in the future. However, if mindfulness overactivates the part of the brain involving awareness of the senses, that can make people fearful should they become oversensitive to every slight change in what they sense.

Expectations Can Lead to Negative Perceptions

Adverse effects, which are lasting negative effects, are not the same as unexpected reactions that do not last. Sometimes people experience something during mindfulness that they label as bad because what happened was not what they thought would happen. They might expect to feel a certain way, like calm, and they might not feel like that. In fact, practicing mindfulness might feel uncomfortable or unpleasant. In one study of mindfulness-based cognitive therapy, 83 percent of participants said they experienced something they labeled as unusual. Britton chalks a lot of that up to expectations. "The unpleasant experiences, or transient stress during meditation, this is also extremely common," Britton says. "Meditation is not always relaxing; people should know that. This can be managed with expectations, what people expect when they come, and just to know that it's not always relaxing."[39]

Expectations that are not in line with reality can be the result of hype. Those who tout the benefits of mindfulness might not say anything about the possibility of negative reactions, even though such reactions are not uncommon. Additionally, people who practice mindfulness and have side effects they perceive as negative, or even have adverse effects, may hesitate to admit it. They may feel like they are doing something wrong or that they are the only ones having that negative reaction.

Some Mental Health Problems Require Professional Help

Additionally, expectations can lead people to believe they can solve their mental health problems on their own with mindfulness, and then they consider the practice wrong or bad when it does not work or seems to make their mental health worse. However, sometimes psychotherapy or other treatment is necessary for psychological issues. Mindfulness meditation is not designed to fix a damaged psyche, although it can be one element in that effort. "Most of the clinical trials that show mindfulness as improving

Mindfulness meditation is not designed to fix a damaged psyche. Sometimes therapy or other treatment is necessary for psychological issues.

symptoms included other psychotherapy 'ingredients' like working through unhelpful thoughts or increasing activity level,"[40] says Jade Wu, a psychologist.

Rande Brown, who is a social worker, thought mindfulness meditation would resolve her anxiety and depression. She studied meditation with a Buddhist master but found she became more anxious and depressed. She would have frightening visions while she meditated, and she felt disconnected from her body. The master told her that her feelings were illusions and she should forget them. She tried, and she continued to meditate but then had a panic attack while walking down a city street. A friend who was both a Buddhist and a psychoanalyst told her she needed a therapist. In therapy, Brown was able to talk about her emotions and her past, something she could not do in mindfulness meditation. Brown says:

"Therapy was able to resolve issues that meditation never had."[41]

—Rande Brown, mindfulness meditation practitioner

> As we began to explore them, I gradually started to feel better and my life-long anxiety symptoms, such as an exaggerated startle response and chronic nausea, disappeared completely. Therapy was able to resolve issues that meditation never had. Over time, I realized that none of my Buddhist teachers had ever really listened to what I had to say. Even with the appearance of a relationship between a meditator and a teacher, when I was performing mindfulness meditation practices, I was basically alone. But with my analyst I was not.[41]

Some feelings of unpleasantness can be common when practicing mindfulness, and adverse effects are a possibility that people should be aware of and seek professional help for if they experience them. However, done in a balanced and moderate way with an awareness of potential pitfalls, mindfulness can help people manage stress and anxiety.

Practicing Mindfulness

Although mindfulness has its drawbacks, it remains popular and effective for many people. The best-known way to practice mindfulness is through meditation, but it is not the only way. In fact, mindfulness can be practiced while just living life. Even simple measures, like paying closer attention to the sensations of breathing or of eating food, can increase a person's mindfulness.

Whichever mindful activity a person chooses, however, that person should embrace seven attitudes, or principles, while doing it, according to a 2024 post by Maggie Wooll appearing in *BetterUp*, a mental health and coaching blog for businesses and individuals. The seven attitudes include observing without judging, patience, being curious and open, trusting one's feelings and intuition, practicing without trying to reach a particular result, accepting what happens in the present without resistance, and letting go of whatever thoughts or feelings are no longer productive to make room for new experiences. The principles were developed by Jon Kabat-Zinn, who created the first mindfulness program.

Breathing

Just breathing is a way to be mindful. This means actually paying attention to the act and sensations of breathing. Paying attention to breathing is not something most people do. For the most part, people breathe in and out every day and every night without thinking about or even noticing what their bodies are doing. Mindful attention to breathing can help people who are experiencing stress, anxiety, and other conditions. Mindful breathing helped Natalie Narvaez when she was coping with major depressive disorder and generalized anxiety disorder, which she describes as "a fear of what's going to happen next."[42] Narvaez had been diagnosed in middle school. Therapy and medication did not produce the improvement she sought. When she got to college at the University of Minnesota, she participated in a study at the medical school there involving mindful breathing and brain stimulation. She got results. "I think mindful breathing had an impact on me—a positive impact—because I've noticed myself being less anxious in everyday activities, taking more time to appreciate little things in my life,"[43] Narvaez says.

"I think mindful breathing had an impact on me—a positive impact—because I've noticed myself being less anxious in everyday activities, taking more time to appreciate little things in my life."[43]

—Natalie Narvaez, mindful breathing practitioner

During mindful breathing, the person pays attention to each inhalation and exhalation. The person considers, for example, how the breath feels inside the body as the lungs fill and expand

Mindfulness can be practiced while just living life. Even simple measures, like paying closer attention to the sensations of eating food, can increase a person's mindfulness.

with air, how it feels when the lungs contract as air is being expelled, and how each breath sounds as it goes in and out. This calms emotions and reduces the release of stress-triggering brain chemicals. "With mindful breathing, they can learn to use their breath as a focus for the present because, with depression, the tendency is to ruminate about past events or about the future,"[44] says Nikita Tavares, who coordinated the study in which Narvaez participated.

Narvaez describes how she goes about mindful breathing. "I close my eyes," she explains. "Concentrate on breathing. Just stay centered with your breathing, so when a thought comes to mind, acknowledge it and you let it go and you come back to the fact that you're breathing and that's pretty much all there is to it—slow breathing for however long you feel you need, grounding yourself, calming yourself down if you're panicking about anything."[45]

Journaling

When Sean Grabowski decided to try mindfulness to reduce the effects of depression, he began with journaling. For Grabowski, journaling was like keeping a diary. In addition to describing what he experienced each day, he also described how he felt about those experiences. This helped him break the cycle of thinking over and over again about upsetting things that triggered stress. "The journaling process helped me catch mental spirals before they gained the power to ruin my morning, day, week, or month,"[46] Grabowski says.

Journaling is relatively easy to do, which makes it a good way for beginners to try out mindfulness. Journaling can be done in different ways. One way to journal mindfully is to use a check-in technique. In this method, people write down daily goals for the week. Daily goals can be related to school or work or home life—or a combination of these. For students, daily goals might include studying for a math exam, narrowing down online sources and books for a history report, completing an art project, or making dinner for siblings one night. Each day, they write about whether they accomplished that day's goal and what emotions they are feeling about their progress.

That method worked to reduce the stress and anxiety Alicia Nortje was feeling. Nortje, a psychology researcher, says:

> I . . . like to jot down hurdles I encountered and describe how I overcame them or whether there is a silver lining to the challenge. As an example, I often feel anxious when I have lots of tasks to complete and don't want to forget about them. Although this is a stressful feeling, I have learned that writing down the list and prioritizing the items is very useful. Now I know that the sense of racing thoughts might be a sign that I have too much work, and I have learned a new technique (list and prioritize) to manage the tasks better.[47]

In other words, check-in journaling helps people think about what they are doing and feeling each day rather than going through their days mindlessly.

Journaling can lead to positive thinking. One form of journaling is to focus on one thing to accomplish in a day. This can include finishing an art project or studying for a test.

Gratitude List

Another form of journaling that can lead to positive thinking is creating a gratitude list. With this mindfulness technique people focus on what is good in their lives in the moment rather than on what is bad. As a result, the brain releases dopamine and serotonin, which are chemicals that make people feel good, and reduces the release of cortisol, which is a chemical that triggers the body's stress response.

> **"One of my most important realizations, is that a lot of the things that you worry about at the time will no longer be relevant to you soon after."[49]**
>
> —Anna Jones, practitioner of mindfulness through gratitude lists

Lisa began to practice focusing her mind on what was good about each day when her mother became ill with pancreatic cancer and then died. "My anxiety increased when going through grief," Lisa says. "There were nights when I couldn't sleep, but then I was thinking of specific things that I was grateful for, that would comfort and calm me so that I could get to sleep."[48] With the help of an app, she has continued this practice of writing daily gratitude lists.

Rather than writing a gratitude list using an app, Anna Jones wrote down things she was grateful for on little pieces of paper each day and then put the pieces of paper in a jar. She would read each piece of paper at the end of the year. Jones says:

> One of my most important realizations, is that a lot of the things that you worry about at the time will no longer be relevant to you soon after. Things that made me feel overwhelmed by stress at work, dates that didn't work out, or feeling low after hearing of someone else's predicament made me realise how [susceptible] to change life really is. After one year of looking back over all the small moments I had to be grateful for, I realised how much of an exercise in mindfulness that keeping a gratitude jar is . . . as much as it can be about helping you to stay in a positive space.[49]

Mindfulness Apps

Although smartphones are often thought of as a source of anxiety and depression, they also are a place where people go to get apps, including mindfulness apps, to find relief from the symptoms of anxiety and depression. Many apps exist, and in recent years scientists have been studying whether they are effective.

More than twenty-five hundred meditation-related smartphone apps have been launched since 2015, according to Appinventiv, a mobile app development company. Calm and Headspace are among the most popular. However, the Appinventiv statistic does not differentiate between mindfulness apps and other apps that focus on meditation.

The question is: Do they work? A 2024 review of twenty-eight research studies of mindfulness apps indicates that the apps work in certain situations. Specifically, people who use mindfulness apps tend to be better at managing their attention and focus, reducing repetitive negative thinking, and being able to observe their thoughts without emotion. The review said results were mixed regarding things like whether people who use mindfulness apps have heightened awareness compared to those who do not, or whether app users are able to remain calm when something happens that would typically make them react emotionally.

Awareness

After beginning his mindfulness practice with journaling, Sean Grabowski moved on to consciously focusing his awareness on the present. He says:

> When I would be doing a knee rehabilitation workout, I would focus on the exercises and each sensation of the experience, and when having conversations, I would focus as intentionally on the individual(s) I was conversing with as [much as] possible. This intensive focus on the experience of the present also helped me to build the skill of letting go of the thoughts in my head as they would arise. Focusing on the present is not easy, but once you develop the skill of detaching from thought, it is something you can do no matter how stressful or taunting those thoughts may be.[50]

Mindful awareness involves experiencing the body's sensations without judging whether those sensations are good or bad. In other words, people pay attention to what they see, hear, feel, smell, and taste rather than go back over old arguments in their minds or worry about upcoming assignments for school or work.

Mindful Eating

One way to practice mindful awareness is through mindful eating. As in the other mindfulness methods, mindful eating involves people paying attention to how their food feels, tastes, smells, looks, and sounds. It is one more way to divert the mind from spending too much time on regrets and worries that can be fuel for stress, depression, and anxiety. Mindful eating involves paying attention to the different colors of the food, for example, and the different textures. Is the hamburger bun squishy, or is it crusty? Does it have sesame seeds, or does it feel smooth? Is the hamburger hot or warm? Is the meat salty, crumbly, or mushy? Is the lettuce on the hamburger cold and crisp or warm and wilted? The idea is to eat slowly and pay attention to all sensations while doing it. If the mind wanders, bring it back to focusing only on the food.

Just like other mindful practices, mindful eating can counter stress because it leads practitioners to slow down enough to feel pleasure, according to the Harvard T.H. Chan School of Public Health. In addition, by slowing down to focus on the sensations of the meal, a person may feel satisfied by eating less than the person would eat if rushing a meal. People who practice mindful eating may find that they enjoy their food more and eat better food because they are paying more attention to what they are eating.

Mindfulness at School

Even at school, a person can be mindful. One way to tune in to the present is to take a moment before starting a test or starting a project to take a conscious breath. This involves noticing the air going in and out, the sound it makes, and how it causes the chest to go up and down and then paying attention to whatever

Who Gets the Most from Mindfulness?

One thing scientists evaluate when they study mindfulness is who gets the most benefit from it. Some studies focus on whether men or women benefit more. The answers have varied.

A 2017 Brown University study of college students who took mindfulness training showed negative emotions like guilt decreased in women more than they did in men, and positive feelings like kindness for oneself increased in women more than they did in men. That does not mean mindfulness does not help men, however. Plenty of men who were part of the study did see their mental health improve, according to Rahil Rojiani, one of the researchers. "Too much data (both anecdotal and empirical) still show how useful and helpful meditation is for men, so our study needs to be seen within a larger context," Rojiani says.

A 2020 study conducted by Rowan University found that men reported suppressing their emotions less after a mindfulness-based stress-reduction program than women did. Mindfulness training aims to get people to be aware of their emotions and accept them without judgment. Men tend to suppress their emotions more than women do, which may explain why men showed a greater decrease in suppressing emotion following mindfulness training than women did.

Quoted in Jennifer D'Angelo Friedman, "Study Suggests Women Benefit More from Mindfulness Meditation than Men Do," *Yoga Journal*, October 7, 2021. www.yogajournal.com.

thoughts come to mind. If the thoughts are negative, like doubts, acknowledge them and then move back to noticing the sensations of breathing and begin work. Do the same thing while working, whenever feeling doubt or fear.

Additionally, slow down. That may seem silly because tests are due at the end of class and assignments have deadlines, so slowing the pace might cause stress. However, speeding through tests and assignments can cause mistakes, and mistakes add to stress. Work at a pace that allows for more efficiency and better-quality results.

Mindfulness Meditation

Of all the mindfulness practices, the one that gets the most attention is mindfulness meditation. Mindfulness meditation can have elements of other mindfulness practices, such as mindful breathing, in which people focus on the sensations of inhaling and exhaling, and mindful awareness, in which people focus on what all of their senses are experiencing. Some other elements, like focusing on the sensations of body parts one at a time, can also be a part of mindfulness meditation.

Mindfulness meditation involves putting aside time to be alone in a quiet place and focusing all attention on the present and on physical sensations. When thoughts intrude that have nothing to do with the present and physical sensations, they are noticed

One way to do mindfulness meditation is to lie down and focus on the sensations of each body part. People often start with their head and move down, or with their feet and move up.

without judgment, and then focus is returned to the present and to physical sensations.

One way to do mindfulness meditation is to lie down and then focus on the sensations of each body part, one at a time. People often start with the head and move down or with the feet and move up. Called body scan meditation, it involves experiencing each body part in the present for a minute and then moving on to another.

Some people prefer a seated position for meditation. While seated they might focus on how their body feels in the sitting position. For example, they might think about how the spine feels against the back of the chair, how their hands feel resting on their lap, and how their clothing feels against their skin.

Walking meditation is another option. With this method, a person might pace a room while focusing attention on the sensations of that movement.

What Else Matters with Mindfulness Meditation

Mindfulness meditation takes practice. When trying to focus on breathing or physical sensations or just being present in the moment, it is not uncommon for the mind to wander. When that happens, the key is to become aware that the thought is there, but not judge it as a good thought or bad thought. Nor should mindfulness meditation be considered a failure when thoughts wander. The goal at that point is to just go back to focusing on breathing or physical sensations or being present in the moment.

Experts in mindfulness meditation suggest paying attention to the amount of time spent mediating. There is such a thing as too much meditation. Studies show that adverse effects seem to coincide with excessive meditation. Scientific studies of several types of meditation indicate effectiveness starts at about ten minutes in a daily practice. Sometimes people meditate for thirty minutes or more each day. Sometimes people meditate twice a day. People who embark on the mindfulness-based stress reduction program developed by Jon Kabat-Zinn and programs like it typically meditate for forty to forty-five minutes daily. Paul Greene, director of the Manhattan Center for Cognitive Behavioral Therapy in New York City, says:

> There is no optimal length of time you should exercise, and there is no perfect number of minutes to meditate, either. With either physical exercise or meditation, it's important that the amount of time you do it be sufficient to challenge you a bit, but not so much as to leave you feeling demoralized or exhausted. Making meditation a regular part of your day is more important than how long you meditate.[51]

How much time a person spends meditating and which method that person finds most helpful are generally a matter of personal preference. "I meditate between 10–20 minutes a day, depending on the day," says Tatiana Posada, an Atlanta attorney who wrote about her mindfulness practice while in law school. "My meditation practice incorporates various styles like mindful breathing, body scans, and loving kindness. I also strive to incorporate mindfulness in my daily routines by trying to be fully present when I'm driving, eating, and walking."[52]

Maintaining mindfulness can be challenging at times. It requires a commitment to practice it most days—if not every day—of the week. It also requires recognizing that the method does not work for everyone and that it is not a cure-all. Mindfulness helps some people, but not others, manage stress and anxiety. A mindful activity that works for one person might not work for another. Mindfulness comes easily to some people and not so easily to others. Some people feel a positive change immediately after a mindful activity, and others do not. Some people experience unwanted side effects, while others do not. While mindfulness has been shown to be helpful to people in managing stress and anxiety, it does not work for everyone or all the time.

There is no perfect time to start being mindful. It can really start anytime, even while eating, driving to school or work, cleaning house, or working at a desk. In all cases the idea is to pay attention to what the senses are registering in that moment and, when a stray thought intrudes, acknowledge that the thought is there without judging whether it is positive or negative. After that, return to being aware of what the senses see, hear, feel, taste, and smell. The payoff can be a greater ability to regulate emotions, focus less on negative thoughts and more on positive thoughts, manage stress and anxiety, and reduce depression.

SOURCE NOTES

Introduction: Living in the Moment

1. Sean Grabowski, "How Discovering Mindfulness at 25 Changed My Life," Mindful Steward, 2025. https://themindfulsteward.com.
2. David Atashroo, "How I Hurt People with Mindfulness," LinkedIn, June 26, 2017. www.linkedin.com.
3. NIH News in Health, "Mindfulness for Your Health," 2021. https://newsinhealth.nih.gov.

Chapter One: Experiencing and Coping with Stress and Anxiety

4. Ellis Edmunds, "My Story," Mindful Therapy for Anxiety, 2025. https://drellisedmunds.com.
5. Quoted in Rethink Mental Illness, "Living with Anxiety and Experiencing Panic Attacks—Becki's Story," July 19, 2022. www.rethink.org.
6. Sophia, "My Sleep Story," University of California Santa Barbara Health and Wellness, 2024. https://wellness.ucsb.edu.
7. Quoted in *Teen Vogue*, "A Day in the Life of a Student with an Anxiety Disorder," 2025. www.teenvogue.com.
8. Quoted in Kathy Katella, "Yes, Stress Can Hurt Your Heart: 3 Things to Know," Yale Medicine, February 12, 2024. www.yalemedicine.org.
9. Quoted in *Alcohol Change UK* (blog), "Martin's Story: 'Alcohol Was the Way I Coped with Anxiety and Depression,'" 2020. https://alcoholchange.org.uk.
10. A. James-Palmer et al., "Yoga as an Intervention for the Reduction of Symptoms of Anxiety and Depression in Children and Adolescents: A Systematic Review," *Frontiers in Pediatrics*, March 13, 2020. https://pmc.ncbi.nlm.nih.gov.
11. Jolanthe De Konig, "Yoga for Stress Relief," BendyLife, May 21, 2021. https://bendylifeyoga.com.
12. Evelyn Acoba, "Social Support and Mental Health: The Mediating Role of Perceived Stress," *Frontiers in Psychology*, February 20, 2024. www.frontiersin.org.
13. Quoted in *Healthy Living* (blog), Mercy Health, "How Do Hobbies Help Mental Health?," April 27, 2023. https://blog.mercy.com.
14. Quoted in Cleveland Clinic, "Why Giving Is Good for Your Health," December 7, 2022. https://health.clevelandclinic.org.

Chapter Two: The Basics of Mindfulness

15. Tatiana Posada, "How Mindfulness Changed My Life: A Law Student's Story," Georgia State University, April 27, 2018. https://news.gsu.edu.

16. Sonya Matejko, "What's the Background of Mindfulness?," Psych-Central, June 13, 2022. https://psychcentral.com.
17. McLean Bolton, "How Does Mindfulness Change the Brain? A Neurobiologist's Perspective on Mindfulness Meditation," Max Planck Florida Institute for Neuroscience, May 20, 2020. https://mpfi.org.
18. Quoted in Rachel Martin, "The Former News Anchor at the Center of the Mindfulness Movement," *All Things Considered*, NPR, July 16, 2023. www.npr.org.
19. Jasmine Abriel, "How I Learned to Love Myself," Medium, August 26, 2022. https://thediaryofjasmine.medium.com.
20. Tariq Maonah, "I Tried Mindfulness at Work with Surprising Results," Medium, December 21, 2018. https://medium.com.
21. Quoted in LawCare, "From Burnout to Balance: My Mindfulness Story." www.lawcare.org.uk.
22. Larissa Bartlett et al., "Mindfulness Is Associated with Lower Stress and Higher Work Engagement in a Large Sample of MOOC Participants," *Frontiers in Psychology*, September 9, 2021. www.frontiersin.org.
23. Quoted in Louisa Kamps, "What Is Mindfulness? Why It Can Be Helpful for Children," Mayo Clinic, August 8, 2023. https://mcpress.mayoclinic.org.
24. Quoted in Pien Huang, "A Visit to One Florida School Where Mindfulness Is Helping Youngsters to Succeed," NPR, January 22, 2024. www.npr.org.
25. Quoted in Huang, "A Visit to One Florida School Where Mindfulness Is Helping Youngsters to Succeed."
26. Quoted in Juliann Garey, "Mindfulness in the Classroom," Child Mind Institute, 2025. https://childmind.org.
27. Quoted in Andy Baggot, "Badgers at Forefront of Mindfulness Training in Collegiate Athletics," UW Badgers, December 17, 2020. https://uwbadgers.com.
28. Shelley La Hay, "Shelley's Story," Centre for Mindfulness Studies. www.mindfulnessstudies.com.
29. Quoted in SensoryEdge, "42 People Comment on the Benefits of Mindfulness," 2024. https://blog.sensoryedge.com.

Chapter Three: Mindfulness Is Not a Cure-All

30. David Robson, "How Too Much Mindfulness Can Spike Anxiety," BBC, February 4, 2021. www.bbc.com.
31. Marco Schlosser et al., "Unpleasant Meditation-Related Experiences in Regular Meditators: Prevalence, Predictors, and Conceptual Considerations," *PLOS One*, May 9, 2019. https://journals.pl.org.

32. Quoted in Sarah Simon, "Too Much Mindfulness Can Worsen Your Mental Health," Verywell Health, June 2, 2021. www.verywellhealth.com.
33. Holly Elmore, "I Believed the Hype and Did Mindfulness Meditation for Dumb Reasons—Now I'm Trying to Reverse the Damage," *Holly Elmore* (blog), July 23, 2021. https://hollyelmore.substack.com.
34. Dawn Foster, "Is Mindfulness Making Us Ill?," *The Guardian* (Manchester, UK), January 23, 2016. www.theguardian.com.
35. Quoted in Robson, "How Too Much Mindfulness Can Spike Anxiety."
36. Quoted in Foster, "Is Mindfulness Making Us Ill?"
37. Quoted in Robson, "How Mindfulness Can Make You a Darker Person," BBC, March 2, 2022. www.bbc.com.
38. Jamie Gruman, "The Times When Mindfulness Could Be Bad for You," *Don't Forget the Basil* (blog), *Psychology Today*, May 11, 2020. www.psychologytoday.com.
39. Quoted in Mindfulness Exercises, "Identifying Adverse Effects of Meditation, with Dr. Willoughby Britton," 2025. https://mindfulness exercises.com.
40. Jade Wu, "What Mindfulness Can (and Can't) Do for Us," *The Savvy Psychologist* (podcast), *Psychology Today*, December 3, 2020. www.psychologytoday.com.
41. Rande Brown, "When Mindfulness Is Not Enough," *Contemporary Psychoanalysis in Action* (blog), *Psychology Today*, March 4, 2019. www.psychologytoday.com.

Chapter Four: Practicing Mindfulness

42. Quoted in University of Minnesota, "Where Discovery Creates Hope." https://wherediscoverycreateshope.umn.edu.
43. Quoted University of Minnesota, "Where Discovery Creates Hope."
44. Quoted in University of Minnesota, "Where Discovery Creates Hope."
45. Quoted in University of Minnesota, "Where Discovery Creates Hope."
46. Grabowski, "How Discovering Mindfulness at 25 Changed My Life."
47. Alicia Nortje, "Journaling for Mindfulness: 44 Prompts, Examples & Exercises," Positive Psychology, July 8, 2020. https://positive psychology.com.
48. Lisa, "Lisa's Story—Appreciation: An Antidote to Anxiety," *Gratitude—the Life Blog*, 2025. https://blog.gratefulness.me.
49. Anna Jones, "What a Year of Using a Gratitude Jar Taught Me About Myself," Medium, September 18, 2019. https://medium.com.
50. Grabowski, "How Discovering Mindfulness at 25 Changed My Life."
51. Paul Greene, "How Long Should You Meditate For? And How Often?," Manhattan Center for Cognitive Behavioral Therapy, November 30, 2020. https://manhattancbt.com.
52. Posada, "How Mindfulness Changed My Life."

FOR FURTHER RESEARCH

Books

Linette Bixby, *Mindfulness Workbook for Teens*. Naperville, IL: Callisto Teens, 2020.

Regine Gallanti, *Anxiety Relief for Teens*. Sydney, Australia: Zeitgeist Young Adult, 2020.

Kristina Dingus Keuhlen, *The 5-Minute Mindfulness Journal for Teens*. Naperville, IL: Callisto Teens, 2020.

Paper Mountain, *The Teen Mindfulness Workbook*. Black Mountain, NC: Paper Mountain, 2023.

Jamie D. Roberts, *Mindfulness for Teen Anxiety*. Naperville, IL: Callisto Teens, 2022.

Nadim Saad and Annabel Rosenhead, *Happy Confident Me*. London: Happy Confident Company, 2020.

Internet Sources

Harvard University, "Mindfulness & Meditation," 2021. www.harvard.edu.

Healthline, "What Is Mindfulness? A Simple Practice for Greater Well-Being," March 29, 2022. www.healthline.com.

Mayo Clinic, "Mindfulness Exercises," October 11, 2022. www.mayoclinic.org.

Mindful, "Getting Started with Mindfulness," November 25, 2022. www.mindful.org.

Psychology Today, "Mindfulness," 2025. www.psychologytoday.com.

Websites

American Academy of Child & Adolescent Psychiatry (AACAP)
www.aacap.org
The AACAP is a professional organization of psychiatrists who treat children and adolescents. It does research, advocacy, and education. The organization's website provides resources for young people who are trying to manage stress as well as for those who have anxiety and depression.

Child Mind Institute
https://childmind.org
The Child Mind Institute is an independent nonprofit organization that provides educational information to families regarding anxiety and other mental health disorders, as well as mindfulness and meditation.

HealthyChildren.org
www.healthychildren.org
This is the website of the American Academy of Pediatrics, a professional organization of pediatricians who treat children and adolescents. Its website provides information regarding the mental and physical health of young people.

Nemours TeensHealth
https://kidshealth.org/en/teens
Run by the nonprofit Nemours Foundation, this site offers information for teens and their families on stress, anxiety, depression, mindfulness and other topics to support wellness of the mind and body.

PsychCentral
https://psychcentral.com
The PsychCentral website provides medically reviewed information regarding mental health.

INDEX

PICTURE CREDITS

Cover: CSNafzger/Shutterstock

5: antoniodiaz/Shutterstock
9: fizkes/Shutterstock
12: Lysenko Andrii/Shutterstock
17: VH-studio/Shutterstock
21: ESB Professional/Shutterstock
23: sutadimages/Shutterstock
29: Larry St. Pierre/Shutterstock
32: Kiefer Photography/Shutterstock
34: MDV Edwards/Shutterstock
40: JeanArteaga/Shutterstock
43: oneinchpunch/Shutterstock
45: DimaBerlin/Shutterstock
50: Serhii Bobyk/Shutterstock

ABOUT THE AUTHOR

Diane Gimpel is a former high school English teacher and a former newspaper reporter. She has written more than a dozen nonfiction books for young readers.